Laughing Through My Depression

VERONICA UTSEY

Copyright © 2018 Veronica Utsey

All rights reserved.

ISBN: 978-0-9994865-1-1

All rights reserved. This book or any portion thereof may not be reproduced or used in any manner whatsoever without the express written permission of the publisher except for the use of brief quotations in a book review. Printed in the United States of America

First Printing, 2018

Perfectly Imperfect Publications
Orangeburg, SC

www.perfectlyimperfectpublications.com

Cover designed by J Ash B Designs
www.jashleybdesigns.com

VERONICA UTSEY

DEDICATION

This book is dedicated to you. You who have gone through and gotten through it. You, currently trying to cope with it. You, who have yet to acknowledge it. You, who have yet to be free mentally and emotionally from it. You, who have found your freedom.

You have a story to tell. It is renewing to release it to the pages of your book or in a speech that you may give, which eventually helps someone else to be released. There's no limit to what you can do. I never thought I'd get to this point in my life, but here I am happily living it. You can do it, free yourself.

Much love to you.

CONTENTS

	Acknowledgments	i
1	Rearview	Pg 16
2	The Quest	Pg 21
3	Still Connecting the Dots	Pg 27
4	Moving Down South	Pg 33
5	Head & Eyes Lowered	Pg 39
6	Shoop Shoop	Pg 41
7	Another Diagnosis & Psych Visits	Pg 45
8	The Awakening	Pg 57
9	Laughing Through My Depression	Pg 63
10	I Am Not My Diagnosis	Pg 66

ACKNOWLEDGMENTS

I thank God for loving *Perfectly Imperfect* me. I know that I am truly blessed beyond my imperfections. I am His Child as I am, as He made me, and as He will make me to be!

Thank you to my parents, Robert Cash Jr. and Emma L. Cash, (R.I.P.) My personality and character traits are a collaboration of both of your bests. Within me, I have and am, the best of both worlds. I am blessed, honored and thankful to have come from and have been loved by you both.

Thank you to my husband, Michael. I attribute the strong foundation that we laid down many years ago to the ability we've had to get through the many losses, roadblocks, and ups and downs. We're still here. I appreciate your love for me and it means more than you'll ever know. You've been a blessing. I love you.

Thank you to my daughter, my "8, 18 or 80," my external heartbeat, Mercedes. You had a front row seat to my journey. Many times, you were the inspiration, encouragement, comfort and drive that I needed. I don't think a mother ever gives birth to a child, looks down at their beautiful face while holding them for the first time and says, "I just gave birth to my best friend," but years later when you began evolving into the woman that you are destined to become, I knew that I had. I am so proud of you! Reign queen! I love you, my gorgeous "8, 18 or 80."

Thank you to my siblings, Valerie, (R.I.P.), Reggie (my older twin) and Venus (baby sis). You are three of my greatest sources of love, strength, encouragement, and my sounding boards. You listened to me countless hours through many mental meltdowns and you never made me feel as if I was infringing on your time. You've been there a multitude of times even when you couldn't understand what I was trying to say for obvious reasons. I am so blessed that you were chosen to be my siblings. You mean the world to me. I love you.

Thank you to my nephew, Corey. During our many lengthy conversations, as we've shared the same spiritual and mental wavelengths, you've inspired and encouraged me. You have a story that you must tell and where we go, you go. People will hear you, near and far. I already know that you stay ready so you won't have to get ready. You will be ready. I love you nephew.

Thank you to my niece, Latasha. Girl, you are one hell of a warrior, queen. The accomplishments that you've managed to achieve while you are battling your health issues are phenomenal! You managed to write three books and have started on two others, all the while dealing with a disabling condition that would have overtaken many. I am so proud of you.

Thank you for encouraging me to write! I love you, my beautiful niece.

Thanks to my sisters from other mothers and misters, Lisa, Feliciaia, Sathia, Sharon and Crystal. You ladies have been a tremendous source of love and encouragement. I've been so inspired by the five of you. Your strength and resilience are amazing. We are six warrior queens, on different journeys, but all prevailing. Reign queens. I love you ladies.

Thanks to my cousin, Hattie P. You always believed in me and my ability to write. You've encouraged me for years and even pretty much fussed at me a couple years ago about getting back to my writing. You have been and are a great source inspiration and love.

Thank you to Ms. Ray. I will forever be thankful for you. You were the reason that I initially realized that I too had a voice. I will always remember how you had confidence in me when I didn't have any in myself. You actually talked to me like I too was somebody who was worthy and able to succeed. I learned a lot from our talks even though it took years for me to begin applying it.

Thank you, Mrs. Martha! You have been and are such a wonderful blessing in my life. For years you have prayed for me, fed my spirit, loved me, and been supportive. You have been a friend, counselor, sister and mother. You've helped me to believe more in myself and you helped align me for the course in my life that I am presently on. I've gained so much from you and there are no words that would ever be enough to express my gratification to you. I love you lady.

Thank you Ms. Kayrine for encouraging me to write and become the servant to my craft with much success. You look out for others and you have a wonderful, welcoming spirit.

Thank you, Mrs. Glover for your friendship, prayers and encouragement. I am so grateful to be blessed with the friend that you've become. It is because of you that I became even more aligned and positioned to live in my purpose.

Thank you to My Writing Coach, Editor, Sister and Friend, Tamika L. Sims. What can I say? In such a short time, you've made a huge impact on my life and I am so thankful and blessed to have been introduced to you. From the first day that I was referred to you and The Self-Assured Woman Community, which was founded by you, I have been positioned more securely to live in my purpose. Thank you so much for creating an online community that many women become empowered, are uplifted and inspired among other Self-Assured Women that become sisters and friends. Also, thank you for believing in me enough to grant me an opportunity to serve as one of the first SAW Ambassadors. Last, but certainly not least, thank you for helping me to successfully birth my very first, "book baby."

Thank you to so many others, whom I haven't named. Charge it to my head and not to my heart. ☺ Proisms are appreciated! I love you.

Introduction

This story is about one woman's journey from being diagnosed with depression and anxiety to her refusal to let anxiety and depression win. This led to her self-healing and strong coping abilities.

She asked herself, *"At what point do I stop letting my diagnosis win?"* If you've tried the many prescriptions, counseling sessions, group therapy and classes and you still have the same diagnosis, then why not try a different **way**?

Come and share in this woman's journey through her life and struggles with a lack of self-confidence and belief in herself which caused her to accept less than she deserved from the people she encountered. Almost giving in to the depression and anxiety, she reached a point where she thought for just a moment that it would be easier to not have to live through it all. It was at that moment that she was awakened and strengthened by a strong sense of self. She realized that she was worth the fight, she deserved better, and she could be and do better. Freedom became a reward that she began receiving and looking forward to even if only in small doses. But it became the drive for her to embrace her walk as she began laughing through her depression.

Disclaimer

This book is one woman's account of how she learned to cope with depression and anxiety, and should not be used to replace the specialized training and professional judgment of a health care or mental health care professional.

Please always consult a physician or a licensed mental health professional before making any decision regarding treatment of yourself or others.

The author, publisher, nor any other contributor to this book is liable for any physical, psychological, or emotional, damages, including, but not limited to, special, incidental, consequential or other damages. You are responsible for your own choices, actions, and results.

Chapter One – Rearview

<u>One Way</u>

As my eyes adjust to the light of day,
The clouds in my mind start to clear away.
Looking over my shoulder I vividly see,
All of the things that sculptured me.
Turning slowly I will glance straight ahead,
Unsure of the road and where I'll be led.
No matter the outcome of my destiny,
The path that I walk was paved for me.

© 2002 Veronica Utsey

All Rights Reserved

Most people will look at and interact with me, but never see the diagnosis of anxiety/panic disorder followed by depression which has been accompanying me on my path in life for more than 10 years. In fact, many would say, "No way," to me having been diagnosed with depression at all. I've been told for years that I have an uplifting voice, I'm Godsent to inspire, I motivate, should start a blog, should write books, I'm hilarious and I make people laugh.

With all of that being said to me by so many different people for years, I know that some of them will have a hard time believing it when they find out that I was diagnosed with depression and have episodes of panic/anxiety attacks, which has been disabling at times. Many of us who are living with these or similar diagnoses know what it's like to *wear it well*. Some of us are great at uplifting, motivating and influencing laughter in others, but when it comes to being that and doing it for ourselves, we are less likely to recognize and apply it for self.

Well I'm here to tell you, I learned how to be uplifted, motivated and inspired in my own presence and I learned to smile and laugh because I finally realized that I am worth fighting my own mind for. I began to encourage and reassure myself and also became familiar with my inner comedienne. That is how my self-healing began.

At one of my weakest points, I was crying so much that the salt from my tears had my face irritated with red splotches that it felt as if it was on fire. My face looked like a very bad makeup application, but I didn't even wear makeup. Sheesh! I cried on the way to work many days during my 45-minute commute, just to end up getting off the interstate to get right back on in the opposite direction to go back home. There were days when I'd make it to work and the tears would begin to fall while I was on the phone with customers and I'd end up logging off and leaving work. Then there were times when I had panic/anxiety attacks that lasted for days. That along with the depression was an impediment to life as it should have been. On one particular day during this period, I'd just gotten back home about two hours after having left for work. I was having an extremely hard morning.

    The tears wouldn't stop falling and I'd had a panic attack that was so rough that I had to pull into a Walmart parking lot to just get myself together to where I felt comfortable enough to drive back home. All I wanted to do was get home, take a Xanax and go to sleep. By the time I made it back home, I was exhausted. I took off the clothes that I'd just put on about three hours prior to go to work, then took the Xanax with water. I got back in the bed and tried to get comfortable. I knew that it wouldn't be long before the Xanax would kick in and I'd be able to be at peace in my medicinally induced sleep.

    Just as I felt myself getting sleepy, I remember thinking, life as it is, is too hard and it'd be much easier to just not live it. Now that in itself made me sit up abruptly. Though I felt extremely tired, I knew I was no longer about to go to sleep. That one quick thought about escaping the difficulties of my diagnoses by no longer living made me take stock of my life and was my wake up call because I was in no way suicidal, nor did I want to die. I was borderline paranoid about and very alert to the possible side effects of the medicines that I had been prescribed. I read all the information provided with prescriptions when they were filled. I would also look up additional information about my prescriptions on the internet.

I constantly checked myself to make sure that I didn't notice mood changes, psychotic or suicidal thoughts as a result of the many medicines that I was taking. It would be funny if it wasn't so sad that the side effects some medicines may cause, really outweigh the benefits that we should get from them. At this point, I was beginning to have another panic attack, but as I was trying to focus on my breathing exercise as an attempt to work through the panic attack I began thinking, "There has to be a different way for me to live beyond the hindrance of these episodes." At that moment, I decided that it was up to me to find a better way to cope with my diagnosis and gain control of its impact on my life.

I got out of bed, went in my den and cried. I fell asleep crying, woke up and cried some more. At this point the tears kept falling as I was mentally formulating a plan to heal on my own. I could all of sudden see just how bad I'd allowed myself to get.

I say all the time that I could be the poster child for *"Perfectly Imperfect!"* I acknowledge and accept my flaws and imperfections and I am living in my truth.

Stigma is one of the biggest reasons why many people don't want to discuss mental health, seek treatment, or admit to diagnosis. I know what it's like to be told by a loved one that my diagnosis, treatment and symptoms are b.s. and I know the feelings of discouragement and hurt that resulted from those things being said to me by one of the persons who mattered most in my life. If you've gone through, are going through or later go through something similar, just know that not everyone that you feel should or would like to be understanding and supportive of you, will be. This doesn't mean that you won't make it through. It just means that particular person won't be there for you while you're growing through it all!

I was told that in order for my story to help someone else that needs to hear it, that I had to be transparent. So I hope that you receive all that you need from my story and that it helps you to gain strength, clarity and confidence to grow through what you are going through. You can do it!

Chapter Two- The Onset

PERCEIVE IT

As indicated by a catastrophe,

Results of are sometimes catastrophic

Cataclysms will make the strongest men cry

As painful realities leave bleeding hearts dry

Born in hope, raised by visions, driven by one's own ambitions

Sometimes one must inhale peace in order to exhale inner agony

Enabling a clear mind to see hope in situations that reek of tragedy

The breaking point can be a conscientious choice to give in by one who is weak

Just as strength is oftentimes more definitive in those thought to be meek

There are some who may see darkness in these words as they read

Sometimes a Blessing is missed because of how we perceive

© 2011 Veronica Utsey

All Rights Reserved

Recently, my life has been playing in the back of my mind like an extended version of a Lifetime movie. Memories that were tucked away, have been coming forward as if to remind me that the past is in part, the reason I am who I am today. I will share some of those memories with you because what I've found is that through the memories, I've been able to connect events from my childhood to the depression and anxiety /panic disorder diagnosis that I incurred.

I can remember when we were at a family member's home and I was three years old. One of the older boys (he was around 10 or 11 at the time), said to me, "Look at my little friend!" Then he told me to touch it and play with it as he placed his hand on mine moving our hands up and down on his little friend. Of course, I later learned that the little friend was a penis. As I look back on that moment I wonder if someone had done the same or worse to him. I also remember that not long after that incident, my mother was babysitting a toddler. I guess he was around the same age as I was then, three years old. We were supposed to be taking a nap. Well I had not too long ago been told to look at and touch a penis, so while she and the boy were napping, I put my hand in his pants and played with his..

My mother woke up, realized what I was doing and popped the hell out of my hand and told me not to ever do that again. I was confused because the big boy said that it was a friend to play with. I quickly learned that maybe it wasn't.

I can remember my older sister laying down looking dazed when I was around six years old. It was weird because I attempted to hit her in the head with my doll as an attempt to make her jump, but she didn't move. For years, I was haunted by that look on her face. I found out later that she had gone through her own trials early in life as well.

I would say that I had a happy childhood. I was very active, played outside a lot with the other children in the neighborhood, and also was imaginative enough to play alone in my room for hours with games, dolls and items that I'd convert for playtime. I remember many times we spent with other family members. We'd go to some of their homes and sometimes they'd come to ours. Other times car loads of family would meet up at a huge park with picnic blankets, lots of food and drinks and much more that would keep us entertained and well fed for many hours. There were a lot of fun family gatherings.

We moved several times. At one of the places that we moved, I can remember my brother having to stack the cushions from the couch in front of his room door at night as an attempt to keep the mice from coming in. Let me just call them what they were. They were rats and I guess they were fat from eating their share of bread. There was a bakery next door and the delicious smell of bread was always in the air, as it was baked fresh all throughout the day. The owner liked my mom so much that he sometimes gave her things for free. One of those times in particular, he gave a large bag filled with bananas.

It was lots of bananas and I ate them until I just couldn't eat any more. I ate so much that a painful rash broke out on the left side of my face by the next morning and I had to be taken to the hospital where they kept me for seven days due to fear of the rash spreading to the inside of my eye. Go figure! From that point, I've not been a big fan of bananas. I was in the hospital on Halloween that year and I remember there was a Halloween party. I guess the staff was trying to cheer us up because what child wanted to be stuck in the hospital instead of out trick or treating. I remember the bumps on my face burning so much and as the other children had mask, I sadly looked up at my mother and said, "I don't even need a mask." That rash had me feeling quite ugly. I can smile about it now as I think about it because of the loving memory of my mother being right there by my side.

Well as you know, young ears hear a lot intentionally and unintentionally. I'm not saying that I was a nosey child, but I can admit that my ears were always up to receiving information for my mind to ponder... I remember hearing about children being beat with an extension cord. Their mom was a friend of our family. I wasn't too familiar with the two children at that time, but then we moved. Shortly after we moved, their mom moved them to an apartment upstairs in the same building. The girl was about a year older than me and the boy was two to three years older!

We played many days together and most times it was upstairs in their apartment. Many times their mom would be in her room just about the entire time that I was up there or not home at all. It was through playing with them that I learned about playing boyfriend and girlfriend. One day when their mother wasn't home, the boy and I were playing a game where we squat down. His sister was watching tv because we were playing as her parents and he'd told her to go watch tv. I don't remember why or how, but the game was played with panties off and I no longer had on any. So we were squatting down with no underwear and all of a sudden I felt horrible pain. The pain was so bad that it felt like I was burning up from the inside. I remember screaming as I fell over on the floor and drew my legs up to my chest.

    He stood there laughing. I remember my breathing becoming difficult as tears were running down my face because the pain was so bad. I know that I didn't lay there like that long, because his sister came running and asking what was wrong. He just stood there unfazed, looking at me. It was hard, but I got up off of the floor holding my legs tightly because it was hurting so bad. I walked slowly and I remember, at one point I stumbled as I was walking out of the door. I slowly made it back downstairs to our apartment. No one was there except my older sister and she wasn't thinking about anything except sleeping.

    When I went in the bathroom I don't know what I was looking for, but I looked down at myself to see if I would be able to see the reason for the pain. I didn't tell anyone because I didn't know what to tell, but I knew the pain lasted for a while. I was around 6 or 7 years old when this happened. I later realized that he forcefully penetrated me by ramming his finger quickly and extremely hard inside of me. That boy later became a grown man who would, under the influence of drugs, rape and murder a young girl. He was sentenced to life in prison where I'm sure he's now being rammed, poked and prodded. My fate could have been so much worse.

    Somewhere within a year of this happening, I remember the daughter of my parents close friends, passed away. Unlike when my grandfather (my mom's dad) passed away, I had my first fears of death, those who died and dying. When granddaddy died, all I remember is that we had to go on a trip, which at the time I could only apprehend as having been a very long ride in the car to a place called South Carolina.

This girl was older than me, but young and died. I never knew what was wrong with her, but I remember that we used to be around her and her parents kind of often.. She was closer to my older sister and brother's age, which would've been around 14 or 15 yrs old. I remember being afraid and looking under my bed after going to her wake. I remember thinking that I wasn't scared of granddad coming back to get me because he would've had to have that long drive to make it to our house to be under my bed. There is where my fear of dying and people who had died began. Many nights as a child, I feared that someone who had died was going to come back to get me and that I would then die too. As I think about it now, I can see how possibly that deep seated fear may have also been a contributing factor of the anxiety disorder.

Chapter Three
Still Connecting Dots

Then there was that time when Santa had a guilty conscience. A slightly older female cousin and I were in her room one day. I was around eight years old, so she was probably around 12 yrs old. She was letting me play with some of her things, which at the time I considered to be big girl toys because she was older than me. I felt special because she was letting me play with her toys. As with some other times in life, good times were ruined by bad actions...

She started touching me inappropriately and it felt so strange because at this age, it had already been established in my mind that boys and girls played mommy and daddy or boyfriend and girlfriend. Not girls and girls, so this experience left me once again confused and feeling weird.

Weeks later her family came to our house and she told me that she had something for me, then she handed me a big envelope. The envelope was addressed to me from Santa Claus at the North Pole. Inside was a book, if I'm not mistaken, a coloring book and some candy. Later after they left, I remember being in my room looking over the envelope and its contents when I realized there was no stamp on the envelope. I knew all about stamps being used to mail letters because we wrote letters to pen pals at school so I began thinking that she must have been Santa, so that left me feeling even worse.

I knew the word "damn" by then and how it sounded when it was used so I angrily thought it... She never touched me inappropriately again, but it stayed with me for a long time.

Some time later, I can remember playing at the home of mine and my older siblings friends. They had a big house and their parents were so nice and always made you feel as if you were one of their own. On this day I was in the kitchen with my friend from school, the son that was my age . I don't remember what we were playing, but we always had fun. He had to go out of the kitchen. I don't remember if someone called him or if he had to go do something. We were in the back of the house so I remember not hearing much as I sat there waiting for him to come back. Knowing me, I was probably playing store or school by myself while I waited. Then one of his older brothers, my brother's friend came in. I remember the way he looked at me and then before I could think anything, he grabbed me, pushed me on the floor, immediately covered my mouth with his hand and was over me with one of his legs in between mine.

I'm trying to scream, but at this point I can't even breathe. I remember trying to breathe, all the while trying to scream, but he was moving so fast. He shifted his body so that he could pull on my shorts. I'm trying to move, trying to breathe, trying to yell. I'm thinking, "Where's my friend? Please somebody help me!" My friend's brother managed to get my shorts partially down and I'm trying to move, but he was putting more of his weight on me. The tears are coming from my eyes. I can't breathe. I see him reaching inside his shorts, pulling himself out. He was trying to penetrate me.

Why is he holding my mouth? Why is he on top of me? I feel as if I'm going to throw up! Oh God! I can't scream. I can't breathe! I can feel him on my skin. He's going to push inside. I'm trying to move, but he's heavy on top of me. He feels hard and he's trying to push inside. I remember that he felt hard and he felt wet down there as he tried pushing into me. I can't breathe. I can't yell or speak. I feel sick. In my head I'm screaming, "Somebody help me please." Then I hear the sound of feet running toward us.

One of their older sisters yanked him off of me. I remember her hitting and yelling at him. I couldn't hear what she was saying. It still felt as if I couldn't breathe. I'm trying to breathe. I remember seeing colors and feeling as if I was going to vomit and fall, but I was already on the floor. She was still yelling at and hitting on him as she backed him out of the kitchen. I remember my friend, helping me up. I think he helped me straighten up my clothes as well. As I release this episode of my life onto these pages, I feel like this one in particular was the beginning of my encounter with panic attacks.

The next thing I remember is my sister coming to get me from the kitchen and walking me home. I was still scared and shaken and could still feel him trying to press into me, even though he wasn't anymore. I don't know if she ever told anyone else, but I know that I never spoke about it. It had become the norm, not to say anything.

My friend and I never spoke of it either, but I do believe that it was him that saved me. I believe he may have come back, saw what was happening and went and got his sister. I was around nine years old. My friend's older brother who was at the time, one of my brother's closest friends, had to have been around 16. I heard many years later that he passed away from complications of a terminal illness. My fate could have been so much worse.

There were so many good and happy days that as a child, I didn't think much of the bad things that sometimes happened to me. I was very active and played hard. In our neighborhood, when we were children, we played kickball, dodge ball, flies up, jumped rope, climb fences, jumped off a high ledge that was behind our buildings, walked and ran up and down the steep hills of our neighborhood and played in the park. There was always something to do and there was never a shortage of energy. We lived in a very diverse neighborhood which was great because people were just people. From what I remember, race nor culture played a negative part in our lives.

There were block parties. Two brothers who lived upstairs in our building were DJs and they would bring their equipment on the street which would be blocked off from vehicle traffic. They'd entertain us with music for hours, while we ate food prepared by the neighbors, play games, and sometimes win prizes. I forgot the man's name that used to turn the fire hydrant on when the temperature reached the 90s and it was muggy hot. We loved to see him coming with that huge hydrant wrench. We'd run to our apartments to ask permission to get wet, then change clothes, get towels to dry off after playing in the water.

During our time in this neighborhood before we moved to South Carolina, I remember watching the news with mama one night, before daddy came home. A story came on about a lady who killed a baby by putting him or her in the oven. The reporter was talking to a neighbor who lived in her building and he was saying how awful the scent was and that it could only be described as burning flesh. He was saying that the lady said the voices were telling her that the baby was the devil. The baby's fate and the vivid description of this horrific event never left me.

There was also the time when a lady that lived on the fourth floor in our building, jumped out of her bedroom window to her death. I was around 9 or 10 when this happened and luckily in the house. I was in my parents room, which faced the front of the building. I was watching tv when all of a sudden I heard screams and then crying. There was yelling, talking and ongoing crying. Not too long afterward there were sirens. The noise lasted for hours. I remember trying to look out of my parents window, which was high even though we were on the first floor. I could see blood and other bodily matter scattered and settling in the cracks of the sidewalk.

Thankfully the steps and the front stoop obstructed my full view because the amount that I did see and the things that I heard had me traumatized. I remember the next morning going back to my parents' bedroom window, looking out. It was Sunday morning and I normally went to the store up the street for one of the neighbors on Sunday morning, but not this morning. There was leftover bodily fluids and matter now mixed with the heavy amounts of water used from the fire hydrant as the police and fire department attempted to rinse her body matter from the ground. This horrific event also stayed with me for a long time and I attribute this to my fear of heights. To this day my fear of heights hinders me from fully enjoying standing on balconies or looking out of windows. Whenever up higher than a second floor level, I have visions of myself and/or others falling. Other people's actions, even when it has indirect negative effects on us, can still ultimately directly affect us!

Mama and daddy now begin talking about moving back home, down south. There are now many boxes being brought home, being packed and stacked. Packing is a lot of work. You find things you hadn't seen in ages. This is when you get to decide on the necessary vs. the unnecessary, what goes and what stays behind. We've all got to choose wisely.

Chapter Four
Moving Down South

We moved to South Carolina in 1980. This is where my parents were originally from. I remember my daddy laughing and saying that people talked different down there and that I would have to get used to it. We had visited quite a few times, but never stayed very long so I never really noticed the difference in lingo. Well there is and I realized what he was talking about after having been down here for about a month.

We prepared for this very long trip and there was much packing to do. We had my dad's big cube truck, my brother's pickup truck and my mom's car. All of the vehicles were packed full and we still had more stuff so there wasn't enough room to bring everything. I hated that we couldn't bring my bike and my noisy hula hoop, but mostly my bike. My big brother built a bike for me. It was red and it looked like a motorcycle. I don't know where he found a motorcycle like frame, but my brother built me the coolest looking bike. No one else had one like it. It was one of a kind and my favorite thing, but it had to stay because there was no room for it. I never forgot it.

The ride was long, hot and tiresome. We made many stops along the way. After what seemed like days, but was only about 14 or 15 hours, we were in front of a house.

At my first glance at the house I thought, "This looks so much different than the houses back home. Where are the neighbors and the steps to go upstairs? Much of our South Carolina family was already at the house waiting for us.

While everyone was taking stuff out of the cars and truck. I remember my daddy and brother were angry because the other truck wasn't there yet, but we're still taking stuff in the house. When I was led to my room, I thought, "This is nothing like my room back home. Can we plug up my tv please? It's hot and I just want to get on the bed and watch tv."

Someone must have heard my thoughts because I don't remember who, but someone plugged in my tv. I'm thinking, "Good! So now I can watch tv." Well it's on, but I'm thinking, "What's all this fuzzy stuff?" I'm changing the station, but there's nothing and so the transition from New York to South Carolina began.

It was summertime when we moved to South Carolina in June 1980. Hot wasn't the word for what it felt like or how it was described. There were many gatherings at our house with the South Carolina family, especially when we first moved. There were many cookouts, lots of food and drinks. Family times were different in South Carolina and in some ways the same.

School was different here. I quickly learned about the haves, have nots and cliques. I wasn't a part of cliques, nor was I to be considered as one of the haves. I didn't dress in the name brands and I didn't have the things that some others had. Feelings of not quite being good enough, you are your materialistic worth and not being a part of the "in" crowd means you're inferior begin to settle in around the age of 11 years old.

When others at school were wearing the new and name brand clothes and shoes and some girls with the popular purses and pocketbooks, I was mixing and matching the same pants and tops to wear them multiple times in one week. The loving lesson that was learned during this time was that the most important thing was that they were clean, and with that appreciation was gained. Yes the fact that I was wearing something more than once in the same week was noted by at least one of the haves who talked about it in class to another of the haves. At the time, I was quietly tolerating being talked about as though I was less because I had already began feeling like I was. At home, our family was very rich in love, but financially, sometimes it was a struggle. I in no way held or hold my parents in any negative light for that. It was what it was. They loved us so that was and is so much greater than any of the things that we didn't have.

When I look back at some of the negatives in childhood, I can only guess that to some, children and teens in the family are easy prey, definite targets because if we all got together and ingested truth serum, many of us would have similar stories to tell about relatives molesting us. So as I got older, there was yet to be more I would later find out through talking with others that many of us were prey to pedophiles, older children, teen relatives, family friends and others who may or may not have been victims themselves in a horrible cycle of molestation.

On my 13th birthday, I remember holding one of the baby cousins. I remember he was only a couple months old and I'm holding his bottle while he's sucking away at the milk. One of my uncles comes over, and caresses the baby's stomach with his fingers while I'm holding him. Then he reaches over and touches my breast, brings his face to mine and kisses me while trying to slip me the tongue. It happened so quick that it shocked me into stillness at first and then I moved quickly toward the kitchen where my aunt was, gave her the baby and sat there with her quietly. I remember taking a deep breath when he left. I never said a word about it, but for the rest of his life, the few times that he was around at the same time that I was, I made sure to go in the opposite direction, careful to make sure that he'd never catch me alone again.

Between the ages of 13 and 14, there was the negotiation. Two relatives who were my senior by 8 and 16 years, the first being one that I looked up too. She had a discussion with the 29-year-old male relative where he told her that he wanted to be with me. They were outside in the backyard as I'm listening from the bathroom window. She says to him that he better not hurt me. What did that mean when you're talking about a 29 year old male and a 13 year old girl? It was all set, I was going to be with a 29 year old male.

I looked up to her so I figured if she says it's ok, then it is. Her boyfriend did not approve of the situation with me and the pedophile. Years later, I saw her then ex-boyfriend in the grocery store and I told him thank you. I thanked him because although he went along with the situation at his girlfriend's insistence, he clearly voiced how wrong he felt that it was. We went on double dates, she with her older boyfriend, me with the older male relative

It became a time of me drinking wine coolers and other alcohol, sitting on the lap of this 29-year-old, being touched by him, and his attempt to penetrate me. My body pushed back and tightened up so much when he tried, that I don't feel that it ever quite happened. This lasted for about a year.

And although I acknowledge that my older sister was wrong in allowing and taking part in this period of my life, I learned that she had also been a victim of molestation and possibly worse in her younger years. I know that what she went through had a very negative effect throughout her journey in life.

During this time she was 20 or 21-years-old. Her boyfriend, if I remember correctly was 39 or 40. A distant cousin was the 29 year old.

I know that my sister always loved me. Years before she passed away, she and I made amends with the differences that we'd had years earlier in life. I forgave her for everything. I loved her wholeheartedly and she loved me tremendously. She became one of my greatest supporters and prayer warriors. She prayed for, inspired and motivated me. She had a heart of gold and loved people. She selflessly gave of herself to help many people in need.

I am so sorry that she endured horrible things in her youth that she may not have lived to make peace with and I'm so sorry that the last years of her life were so difficult. I told her on many days, as I tried to motivate her while she was bedridden due to illness, that she deserved so much more in life, free of the hindrance of her then health and body.

I told her that she deserved to be free to do all of the things that she wanted to do, happily, healthily with an abundance of love and that she could and would do it. I had faith that she would and for a short period she was doing it before her health failed again which led to her passing away. As I write this right now, through the tears falling from my eyes at 1:00 in the morning, I just hope that she knew just how truly loved she was. R.I.P. Big Sis! I love and miss you so much. You would've been so proud of me. I can see your beautiful smile and hear you say, "You go baby! I knew you could do it!"

Chapter Five-
Head and Eyes Lowered

The final occurrences of inappropriate acts against me as a child were with the male relative that would sometimes stay the night at our house. Our house, should have never meant my room. He'd creep into my room late at night to fondle and hump on me. I was 14 years then and wondered if this was how it would always be. About a year after this began, it all stopped. We moved to a much smaller house and for a long while there weren't any family gatherings at our home.

At this point, I knew how to dodge the pedophiles and overly touchy feely family members and others. It also didn't hurt that a couple months before my 16th birthday, I became girlfriend of a, "not so small football player," who later became my husband. I guess his football playing size could be intimidating and also deter some of the most persistent predators. I lived many years silently enduring so much less than I deserved and went through a long period of my life just accepting whatever came from whomever.

Sometimes the most negative things that we go through in life have a way of following us for years after they've happened. As a teenager who was raised in a loving home with siblings and both parents, there was much happiness and love. Yet I walked with my head and eyes down. No matter how great the love, there was enough that transpired outside of the circle of my immediate family that even before I learned about worth, my own had less value to me. I didn't feel as if I was good enough to associate with people that I, at that time saw as better.

I didn't think I would ever be able to accomplish many of the things that others had and would. I honestly felt inferior to some people and I realized that I had for most of my life. I encountered many people who treated me as though I was less because in their eyes I had less, so to them, obviously I was less. Today I realize that those thoughts of how I felt that others felt about me could have been fueled by my own feelings of low self-worth.

Money wasn't plentiful in our house. In fact, a couple years after we moved to South Carolina, money became scarce. Financially, there were some pretty hard times especially during most of my middle and high school years. I didn't want to look anyone in their eyes because I didn't want to see the pity, superiority, or ridicule that I felt would be reflected in their eyes when they'd look at me. As I got older, I also didn't want them to see the sad story that was sometimes evident in my eyes. I went through much of my life avoiding eye contact and trying not to be seen.

I walked with my head down as a way not to be noticed. I hated being seen and dreaded attention being drawn to me. There have been times in the last several years that my husband pointed out to me that he knew what I was doing when I wouldn't get up if we were in the presence of others, especially out in public. He saw that I would still sometimes try to avoid being seen.

Chapter Six-
"Shoop Shoop," The Greatest Loss

Forever Tied

On the day I was born, I screamed and cried
My Umbilical cord severed we were no longer tied
Pushed from your womb and the beat of your heart
My lifeline and me were suddenly apart
Placed in your arms the tie was brand new
For 27 years God blessed me with you
Severed again and once again I cry
Now you comfort me with a new eternal tie.

© 2001 Veronica Utsey

All rights Reserved

Mama called the week before Thanksgiving of 1995. She asked that we come to their house for Thanksgiving. The way that she asked felt different, that there was no way that we weren't going. That Thanksgiving turned out to be the best. The only thing that would've made it better would've been my brother and his family, who lived in New York, being there with us. We had a great time. It was my parents, my older sister and her two sons, my younger sister and her boyfriend, my husband, our daughter and myself, along with a few other family members. The most memorable time while we were there was when my mom, along with my two sisters and my daughter, who was only four at the time, and I started singing, Whitney Houston - Exhale (Shoop Shoop) along with the song as it was playing. We had so much fun singing and laughing together during this song that we all loved. The funniest part was that mama kept coming in late when singing the "Shoop Shoop..." part of the chorus so we would bust out laughing every time she did it so we laughed through most of the song. I hate that day ever ended.

Two days later, early on that awful Saturday morning after Thanksgiving 1995, we would be awakened by a call from Daddy who could barely speak through his sobbing that Mama was dying and that the EMTs were trying to revive her. We jumped up out of bed, rushed to make it to their home, was stopped by the police because my husband was speeding, through tears I told the police officer what was happening, he made a call which confirmed it quickly for him. Then he let us go, telling us to be careful. On the way to their house, we passed the ambulance which was going in the opposite direction toward the hospital. They were going slow, no siren, just the lights flashing. I already knew her fate.

She was gone! The hole in my heart that losing my mother left was big enough for me to bleed to death. My lungs felt as if they were closed. It felt as if my chest was being crushed. I couldn't breathe. It felt like I was submerged in quicksand, it was so hard to move.

My mother was the heart of many and so many people felt and still feel the loss that resulted from her death. For weeks after she passed, mentally I had to place her on a much needed, much deserved vacation. I couldn't accept that she was gone. It felt like I was living outside of my own body as I looked on at the shell of who I was moving about day by day crying, hyperventilating, sad and hurting, still not quite believing and not fully functioning mentally or physically. The pressure on my chest was so heavy that it was difficult to breathe and move. I finally went to the doctor. I was diagnosed with anxiety and was told that I was having panic attacks. I was prescribed two medicines and sent on my way.

Months went by, the panic attacks began coming in less frequently, the fog began to clear and then I had to slowly start dealing with the fact that my mother was actually gone. I never knew how strong I could be until I began to face my greatest loss.

Several years passed and I noticed that every hardship, negative, sad or stressful moment that I experienced affected me much worse than it used to. At home, at work, other people's problems or tragedies, everything that wasn't good or positive had a harsh effect on me physically. Stress was causing painful flare ups. By this time, I'd been diagnosed with Interstitial cystitis (an incurable, autoimmune disease which causes chronic pain), degenerative bone disease (osteoporosis) and migraines so I now had on top of anxiety medicine, medicine to treat the cystitis, migraine and pain meds for all three. I'm paranoid about side effects from medicine so I read the info that comes with prescriptions.

Sometimes reading the side effects would cause a panic attack. Yes that! At this point, I am only taking one medicine consistently and that is the one for Interstitial cystitis. I refused to take the others on a consistent basis for fear of tempting fate with the opportunity to serve me some of the severe side effects from any of the medicines. Also, my thinking was and still is, if I'm taking several different medicines consistently over a period of time then I risk being affected by negative drug interactions.

I was now going to the doctor more often and constantly getting different prescriptions. When I would say that I'm not taking the medicine, to the doctor it meant, "Let's try you on something new!" This went on for a couple years as life began serving up more stress.

Chapter Seven-
Another Diagnosis and Psych Visits

"I'm Coming Home"

Sometimes we are better presenters than we are receivers...

Oftentimes, one picture has so many different meanings....

Never is truth the same for all envisioning it...

One man's right will always find a way to be another's wrong...

Love and happiness, Hurt and pain are universal, but not the same...

There are Reasons and Causes, Actions and Reactions...

Righteousness has roots that goes way back in time...

Justification has limbs that grow weak and fall through time...

Every good and bad moment has a season and will pass...

Maybe we should live every minute like it is our last...

© 2011 Veronica Utsey

By 2011, I was missing a month or months at a time from work. I'd had a number of EAP (Employee Assistance Program) scheduled counseling visits as well as insurance covered counseling visits and I was still having a very hard time. My life had become physically painful and overpoweringly stressful. Between the chronic pain from cystitis, migraines and arthritis I was in pain much of the time. Relationship issues and work were also causing considerable stress that contributed to my physical pain and wreaking havoc on my skin.

I'd been crying so much, extremely tired, couldn't concentrate on anything, and was having constant panic attacks. It was time to go to the doctor again. I was always getting reprimanded for not taking my medicine. Well I wondered if the doctors read the possible side effects of each medicine that they prescribed and thought whether or not the ends justify the means when looking at the possibility of drug interactions and/or severe side effects especially when prescribing multiple medicines.

I remember this particular visit to the doctor. My eyes were red from crying and my face has red splotches that were irritated from the salt in my tears. My eyes were holding the tears until I was placed in the room to wait for the doctor. Once in the room, the nurse began to ask routine questions. I was trying to hold the tears back, but they began sneaking out of my eyes, down my face.

My face was screaming from the stinging caused by the tears, but I tried to act like I didn't notice while trying to spot the tissues so that I could get one without the nurse noticing and wipe my eyes. I was tired of crying and tired of my tears betraying me in front of other people. I was tired of my eyes and my face telling my business. The nurse handed me the box of tissues, and I was so frustrated with my eyes for leaking.

The doctor comes in, the nurse stays put and she begins relaying to the doctor my answers to the questions that she'd asked me, some of which I didn't even remember answering. By this time, I have two handfuls of wet tissues. Between my running nose and leaking eyes, I looked a hot mess. Then she asked how long I'd been experiencing the symptoms. As I answered, I started crying. I broke. I mean snotty nose, lip quivering, out of breath crying. They removed the tissues from my hand and placed the box of tissues back in my hand. The nurse actually cooed and wiped my face. They waited the few minutes for me to calm down and then the doctor said, "You are suffering from depression."

Immediately, the tears were flowing like a faucet and I was crying to the point of being out of breath again, gasping and hiccupping as I said in denial, "No I'm not!" I was a blubbering mess and It's actually kind of funny as I think back on it now, but definitely not then.

Now, there's additional medicine, two prescriptions for depression. I tried them even though the side effects scared me because after talking to the doctor that day, I felt that maybe the medicines would help. That was short lived because my body has a very low tolerance to medicines and what should've taken weeks to get into my system, affected me fairly quickly. I was out of work for about a month and the medicines kept me in an overly relaxed mode. I slept much. I really wasn't functioning and wasn't getting much done.

It was then time to go back to work. I had an hour drive, both ways, to and from work so I couldn't be medicated, especially while having to drive, even without medicine in my system, I'd had problems with falling asleep while driving. I was looking forward to getting back to work and back to my normal routine, minus all the crying.

I got back into the swing of things at work. I was doing pretty well for a while. I had some difficult times managing the depression and anxiety. The panic attacks were less frequent for a while. I had what I called, "heavy hitters" for pain and depression along with one for migraines that you couldn't pay me to take regularly. Well about one and a half to two years and much stress later, depression and anxiety were pulling rank again. I finally went to a counselor that suggested a four to six week outpatient treatment program. The counselor completed the necessary paperwork and I was out from work yet again.

The first day at the outpatient program was busy with evaluations, appointments and then the initial group therapy/learning session. It was strange being in a room with people who were there because they were experiencing similar symptoms.. As I peeped up at faces every now and then I thought to myself, they all look as normal as I perceive myself to be. They were mothers, fathers, grandparents, managers, employees, employers, different levels of education, income, and social status. I'd been told in no uncertain terms that I was only claiming to go through what I was going through and that it was all b.s. On this day, in this room, with these other normal people from all walks of life, it was confirmation for me that it wasn't just real for me, but that mental disorders including but not limited to depression, PTSD and anxiety were also very real to many others as well.

We had classes, counseling and psychiatric appointments. I was still commuting because the program was in the same city that I worked in so this was a tiring all day, five day a week program. The psychiatrist and nurse convinced me to begin taking the hydroxyzine again by telling me that it's the medicine that was used with children before surgery and giving me the lowest dosage so I was taking it at night.

So weeks later, the last day of class and those that are left have become a small family. That day was hard because one of us was being told that they may need to be admitted to inpatient, several of us didn't feel they were ready to be done with the program and we were all going to miss each other. I was ready to take some of what I'd learned and apply it to life, but it was bittersweet.

Chapter Eight-

The Awakening

"In Too Deep"
When I lay my head down, my mind begins to soar
It's like an overflowing river, bringing everything to shore
The troubles in this world are easy to see
As I look at the worn I envision them as me
I am the weak, the sick, the poor and the torn
My child is dying, my heart is heavy, my soul is worn
As I look for relief, there is none in sight
Oh God please help me, I'm too weak to fight
My fellow man is at war, he doesn't have a clue
He thinks money is his answer, he's confusing it with you
Division is our downfall, we should have all been "ONE"
If words were the ultimate weapon, there'd be no gun
Man worships money, he is blind and can not see
I am the addict, the exploited, the fearing, the lost
Power is to be claimed and I am the cost
As my mind slowly shifts, I am allowed a moment's peace
I see a world with no borders, jails or police chiefs
Scientist and doctors together roll up their sleeves
United to heal the sick and cure every disease
Children are happy as they learn and play
Acquiring good values and morals everyday
Nobody's left homeless, hungry or alone
Together we are one, we are stronger than stone
The alarm clock snatches me from a restless sleep
As reality approaches, I'm mentally "In too deep!"

© 2006 Veronica Utsey

All Rights Reserved

4th quarter 2014, it's back to work I go. I'm feeling better and ready to get back into the swing of things. The closer I got to work on that first day, the more I could feel the queasiness in my stomach, flutters in my chest and the tightening feeling in my shoulders. Stress! It had become the norm for my body to react to stress. My job had become a major source of stress. Driving back home, at times I would have the same symptoms. I was now stressed when loved ones were stressed and also as a result of the tragedies that happened, locally, nationally and internationally. It felt as though I could feel everyone's pain.

I made it to work, grabbed ahold of my sanity as I gathered my pocketbook and jacket before walking into the building. One foot in front of the other, I focused and made it off of the elevator. That's how I made it through the day. I took one step at a time. By the end of the work day I was back in tune with my job.

Days went by, some better than others, as with everyone else. I was back, but there was a feeling deep inside that something was coming. I stopped with the hydroxyzine and was rarely taking the Ativan because I was now taking Xanax for those harder to manage panic attacks. I'd only taken three doses of the depression med that was prescribed on the last day of the outpatient program. I was done with it too.

Several months later, I would jump up out of bed panicked because it felt like I couldn't breathe. I would have a hot and cold feeling and sometimes start shivering from the cold sensation. This had happened in the past, but the episodes had gotten more severe. I'd realized that whenever this would happen that my pressure would be very high so I'd grab the blood pressure monitor to check my pressure. Each time it was confirmed high, sometimes I'd try to make it to the den or frantically call out to my husband. Other times I'd try to fight it until it would eventually subside. A couple times it was so bad that my husband took me to the emergency room in which they'd administer an EKG, check all of my vitals, sometimes they checked my blood, but these visits always resulted in them giving me a shot of Ativan which immediately relaxed me and put me to sleep. The doctor would always say that I needed to take the medicine that I'd previously been prescribed for anxiety and depression. Then they'd send me home.

A few times my husband called 911. The paramedics would get there, check my vitals while asking questions. After confirming that my pressure was high and that I was indeed probably having a panic attack. They'd offer to take me to the hospital, which I'd decline so they waited until it calm down to a level that they were comfortable with then they'd leave, but not before telling me that I needed to take the anxiety and depression medicine.

This all had become my life. I wore it well because only those that witnessed it would believe it. Very few people actually knew what I was going through. My supervisor was one of those that knew. On one particular morning, I was pretty upset so I was already going through it before I left home. As soon as I got on the interstate, the tears started falling. I was trying to make it to work. I didn't want to miss another day from work, but I received a phone call that upset me even more.

When I got off of the phone I was crying. I kept wiping my eyes and nose and I had no idea when I got off of the interstate, but I all of a sudden didn't see anything familiar. I drove a little further down a road that seemed to be long, pulled over on the side and called my supervisor. I was so upset, tears still falling and trying to catch my breath. When she answered, I crumbled. I was able to say her name and then there was a long pause after she said mine because I couldn't speak. The tears were constantly falling and I was trying to calm down enough to speak.

Finally, I was able to say I can't come in today. She knew that I was crying and is truly concerned when she asked me what was wrong. I knew it was difficult for her to understand what I was saying because I was still crying, but then she asked, where I was and I cried as I said, "I don't know!" I'm crying even harder at this point as she's trying to help me to figure out where I am. She stayed on the phone with me until I calmed down and my brother called me. I had to convince her, before she would get off of the phone, that I was ok, was going to use GPS, talk to my brother on the way home, text her to let her know that I made it safely, then take a Xanax and go to bed.

By the time we got off of the phone, my brother had hung up so I used the GPS until I got back on a familiar road, pulled over in a Walmart parking lot, took time to breathe and get myself together. I then got back on the interstate headed towards home, wiping at the few tears that were still occasionally falling. I called my brother back. He already knew from the way I sounded that something was wrong. He didn't press me for details because knew that I was already upset. He stayed on the phone with me until I got home and in the house and I promised him I'd be ok, that I was going to take a Xanax and go back to bed.

This is when as I felt myself getting sleepy, I remembered thinking, life as it is, is too hard and it'd be much easier to just not live it and that caused me sit up abruptly. I was so tired from the events of the morning, but knew that I would no longer be able to go to sleep immediately at that time. The thought of dying just to escape the difficulties of my diagnoses woke me up and made me take a good look at my life as it was and I was not pleased with the reality that I saw. I wasn't suicidal nor did I want to die. Trying to fight the panic attack that this thought was causing, I began thinking, "There has to be a different way for me to live beyond the hindrance of these episodes." At that moment, I decided that it was up to me to find a better way to cope with my diagnosis and gain control of its impact on my life.

As I stated previously, I got out of bed, went in my den and cried. I fell asleep crying, woke up and cried some more. At this point the tears kept falling as I was mentally formulating a plan to heal on my own. I could all of sudden see just how bad I'd allowed myself to get.

I decided at that moment that depression, anxiety, neither panic attacks would continue to have control over my life. It was time to take it back.

Chapter Nine-
Laughing Through My Depression

Of Him

As I listen...and read between...invisible lines....in my mind I see things. That to my eyes I am blind...Too strong...to be broken...Spirit so sublime...and yes if you're wondering...these words are mine... Weathering storms...encouraging growth... motivating uprising.... knowing my worth...seeking wisdom... At the same time... I wipe away tears... that may have been for...your pain... not mine....I can do and be all things...because God's truth is mine…

© 2010 Veronica Utsey

All Rights Reserved

Through the years I'd been told by several doctors, and counselors that depression and anxiety would be a part of me for the duration of my life, but that it was treatable. That was a heavy reality for me. It felt like a sentencing. I'd already been told the same about the Interstitial cystitis and arthritis and I wasn't quite sure how to accept yet another life sentence.

I sat there thinking about the panic attacks, anxiety, depression, the medicines and counseling. The outpatient program and the fact that I was still not any better. Then I asked myself, if you've tried the many prescriptions, counseling sessions, outpatient therapy and you still have the same diagnosis, then why not try a different way?"

The first thing I did was stop taking all of my medicines. I realized that there were warnings against stopping some of the medicines abruptly, but at that moment I wasn't willing to deal with the side effects of continuing to take any of them. I was tired of being tired and I felt like I was much stronger and more able to fight panic attacks and depression without having medicine in my system. I felt that my mind had been leaning too much on the promises of the medicine making things better. In essence, I felt that my mind had gotten too dependent on a substance that was only meant to assist with what was considered a mental disorder. Acknowledging all of that, I now knew that I would have to fight my own mind for control over my own life.

As I thought about that, I started laughing. I was laughing because it was strangely comical to me that I had to battle my own mind for my mind. I walked to the mirror, looked myself into the eyes and said, "Game

On!" Though this was a very real life situation for me, I felt that the whole scene was comical, but as I looked at my own image in the mirror I wasn't smiling. I then realized that I couldn't remember the last time that I genuinely smiled, so I smiled. It was so awkward looking at myself in the mirror trying to smile. I stood there looking in the mirror for about forty five minutes trying to see myself genuinely smile. I started laughing again. I was laughing because it was funny. I thought I had quite possibly forgotten how to smile. I decided then that I would use the mirror as a tool to smile and laugh more, but to also check myself on how well my inner victories would reflect outwardly. I became even more determined.

Mentally I began a list of things that I would do to grow through what I'd gone through. I thought back to the last phone call with my supervisor when I didn't know where I was. I started laughing again. By this time my eyes were running because I was laughing so hard. I told myself that I was a blubbering idiot and I laughed some more. I knew then how I was going to get through depression and anxiety. While I was going to be fighting my mind for my own mind I was going to also be laughing through my depression and anxiety.

I started positive self-talk, a therapy takeaway. Whoop Whoop! I started telling myself often that I am not my diagnosis. I will get better. I will get control over my life. I can, I will. There was so many more positive things that I said to myself. I began to see humor in just about everything and I laughed so much more. I made myself look into the mirror daily to just smile and soon it became natural. I still laughed at the fact that I had to learn to smile again.

As much as I would encourage and motivate others, which I loved being able to do, I made sure to encourage and motivate myself from this point as well. I must say that it was still much easier seeing the possibilities and triumphs to come in and for others than it was for me to see for myself, but I was determined to be just as good in this aspect for myself as I knew that I was for others. Honestly, when it came to self-talk and self motivation, when I first began this journey of battling my own mind, I didn't believe all of the positive things that I told myself and some days it was extremely hard to follow through, but once I convinced myself that I was worth the fight, I refused to lose and quitting or going back to the way it had been was no longer an option. I made sure that not a day went by without my positive self-talk and motivation. On my worst days, I was even more determined to speak something good into and about it. The more I did this, the easier it became to do.

As I grow, I gain... I was starting to feel stronger. The stronger I felt physically, the better I felt about myself. I was gaining power over me. I began interacting with people differently. I became a little more sociable, but I also became more direct. The days of me tolerating words or actions meant to belittle or weaken me was over. I was fighting for me and refusing to lose. I now knew for sure that I was just as worthy as any and everyone else.

And then there was the night... Whack! I jumped up out of my sleep. I couldn't breathe. I felt the tingling in my arms and had that hot and cold feeling at the same time. I sat on the side of the bed and felt like I was going to pass out. I grabbed the blood pressure monitor, checked my pressure and of course it was high. I sat there trying to calm it down. At this point it had been about three months since I'd taken any meds so I was completely alert to every physical sensation that I was experiencing, but I refused to consider taking anything.

I struggled to stand up, my body felt like lead. I sat on the floor because for me, breathing was a little better when I was down there. Of course, this time it wasn't working. I'm attempting the breathing technique that I'd learned in therapy. Whoop Whoop! Nope. It wasn't working. I grabbed onto the bed and pulled myself up.

I could hear the tv in the den playing, and wasn't sure my husband would hear me over the sound of it. I called out, which was more like a whisper because I was having trouble breathing. I made it to the living room and called his name again. This time he heard me. He came to see what was wrong as I made it back to the bed. He already knew what was happening. I told him I felt like I was going to pass out and I may need to go to the hospital. He called 911 while getting ice and began wiping my face and neck with a washcloth wrapped in ice and drenched in cold water. I started shivering real hard to the point that I was shaking. He opened the door for the paramedics.

At this point they were familiar with me so they came to my bedside, checked my vitals and one of them says, "Yes. You've gotten yourself into a frenzy this time. You've got to work to calm it down." I was still shivering hard and trying to focus on my breathing exercise. So the three of them, (my husband and the two paramedics), are standing there trying to talk me into a calmer state. Then one of them ask, "Are you taking your medicine?" I shook my head, no. I could see through my peripheral vision that he was shaking his head at my answer.

At this point I could feel myself coming down from the panic attack, but I'm giggling on the inside because when I peeped up at them, I see three slightly ticked off faces because of my answer of "no" to the question about if I was taking the medicine. I'm giggling inside because, even though one of them on a previous call out to my house had admitted to being diagnosed with anxiety disorder and spoke about how the medicine was helping her, I knew that wasn't going to be my story. I was also giggling because I thought that maybe they thought that this and the other times they came out could've been avoided if I'd just take the medicine, which I knew that I was done with.

It was getting hard to hold the laughter in as I'm still seeing a little frustration at my answer on their faces. I smiled at them and told them that I was feeling better and to please give me a few minutes to get myself together. The three of them went in the living room and my husband closed the room door so that they could sit and chat as they had gotten used to doing and I could sit up and get myself together.

By the time I calmed completely down and slipped something on, I was exhausted, but feeling triumphant because I had come through and had no medicine in my system. I was winning my mental battle.

That was the last time that they were called to come see about me. It's been about two and a half years since I've had a panic attack even a fraction of that magnitude.

Chapter Ten-
I Am Not My Diagnosis

It has been a very long and eventful journey that I am still on. There's been many ups, downs and losses. At this point in my life I'm coping, but every now and then, the tears break through the armor-like wall of strength that I've built and spill from my eyes.

When my strength is low and I'm feeling slightly broken, I self motivate first. There are cracks in this armor. I'm Perfectly Imperfect, but I refuse to take any more just laying down in defeat! I am not my diagnosis and you aren't yours. We are not the things that we've gone through or things that we've done.

With that said, tears have fallen at times, but I wipe them and keep it moving. I've got too much to do and I just can't give in and let it win. No daily meds. No counseling. No classes. Been there, done that! Same diagnosis...sooo I've been keeping it positive. Constantly affirming to myself that I'm strong enough, well enough, good enough.

To you, me and all of us...We've Got This!
We can and we will grow through what we go through...

Bio: Veronica Utsey

Veronica Utsey was born in New York and raised in South Carolina, or as she so pridefully says, she is, "Northern Born and Southern Seasoned." She's an author, an Independent Business Owner of Ronni's 'Razzi' Jewelry boutique and Founder of "Truth Be Told" Facebook community. She is certified in Mental Health First Aid and her mission is to empower others to, "Move from Panic and Anxiety to Power," through inspiration, motivation and coaching. Her goals are to become an Award-Winning Author, Motivational coach and Speaker. She lives in her truth that she is, "Perfectly Imperfect!"

Veronica loves traveling and spending time with family. Her favorite place to be is at the beach and she enjoys writing, reading, listening to music and drinking tea! She also acknowledges that we can learn something new every day and are elevated through the love and support that we receive from others, so she adamantly believes throughout life, "It takes a village!"

My Passing Of The Torch To You

Whatever you've gone or are going through, just know that it's never too late to grow through it!

My way worked for me, but within you is the answer to what will work for you. No matter what your means of getting through what you're going through, just be dedicated enough to YOU to get to your breakthrough.

You CAN do it and you ARE worthy and deserve it!

I am passing this torch to you… Receive the Winner's Torch and Run With It!

Make it to your breakthrough, then pass it on!

Your new beginning starter workbook is included…

Go! Take your control back!

VERONICA UTSEY

NEW BEGINNING

WORKBOOK

Write a brief summary of your life from childhood to now (Include the good and not so good)!

LAUGHING THROUGH MY DEPRESSION

Try to connect dots from some of the things that you experienced, including during childhood, to how you are today!

What are you going through that you want to get through (diagnosis, situation or circumstance...it doesn't have to be medical)?

Fill in the blanks with your personal terms!

_____Through My _____!

NOW

What are you going to do to get through what you're going through? Think about it as you go to the next page!

**You're doing great!
You can do this!**

What are some steps that you are going to take to get through what you're going through? Create your "To Do" list!

(Begin with filling in your blanks and then go to the next page to jot down some of the steps you will take.)

_____Through My _____!

You are truly worth fighting for!

You are going to win!
My "To Do" List

Now Map It Out! Put your to do list into a schedule format, daily, weekly and/or monthly... You may choose to use all three schedule formats.

Now you are on your way. Your first step is the hardest, but you must take the step. This journey won't be easy, but it will be worth it!

Laugh more! Smile more! Celebrate your victories! Get back up from your falls! Just Keep Going!

Somebody right now is waiting for you to win and then share your journey so that you can pass them the winning torch!

You can do this! Pass on the winning torch!

LAUGHING THROUGH MY DEPRESSION

www.ingramcontent.com/pod-product-compliance
Lightning Source LLC
Chambersburg PA
CBHW060420050426
42449CB00009B/2056